Norwegian Forest Cats and Kittens

Care, Nutrition, Behavior, Personality, Health, Training, Breeders and more (Official Cat Owner's Books)

D1157607

By Clare Smiley

Contents

Norwegian Forest Cats and Kittens

Contents

For my beautiful cats

Kevin and Lucy

Contents

Contents

Introduction

I want to thank you and congratulate you for buying this book, **"Norwegian Forest Cats and Kittens"**.

The book contains proven steps and strategies on how to **pick out and raise a Norwegian Forest cat for showing, breeding or as a loving companion.**

Inside this book you'll discover things like...

- How to select the best cat from the breeder by asking these questions that most people forget.

- What age you can bring them home and why some breeders want you to wait.

- The easiest way to make sure your cat settles in perfectly and doesn't get stressed.

- Essential health tasks that you may not realize about the Norwegian Forest cat

Introduction

- What you must check for regularly (and importantly what not to do)

- Specific health issues found in the Norwegian Forest cat (and how to check for it)

- A great tip for selecting a really good vet (and what to look for)

- Understand their behavior and why they do certain things

- How to stop different types of bad behavior the easiest way.

- Help them cope with shyness and fear

- Discover how to train them like a professional

- What you need to win at the shows

- Breeding? Here's what you need to know for best results

- If you ever have to travel with your cat you'll need this guide

and so much more...

Introduction

I know there are other 'Norwegian cat books' on the market. But I really have tried to give you everything you need to know in one place.

If you love the companionship of cats, you will love learning more about the Norwegian Forest Cat. Learn about its humble origins, its playful personality and how it can fit into your home to become a loving, faithful cat companion. By the time you finish reading this book, you will want one of these beautiful creatures in your home to love and adore.

Thanks again for reading this book, I hope you enjoy it!

Chapter 1 - The Origins of the Norwegian Forest Cat

Although its name sounds as if you would find a wild animal out in the woods, the Norwegian Forest cat isn't a dangerous predator. It is a type of domestic cat. With its long, thick fur, this cat is content in the coldest regions of the world and it is a popular breed in the coldest areas of Northern Europe. As the name implies, it can be found in homes in Norway, Sweden, Northern France and other cold regions on the continent.

The Skogkatt, which means "forest cat" in Norwegian, is believed to have appeared on the continent thanks to the Vikings. The exact origin of the Norwegian Forest cat is uncertain, as many believe that it was developed by longhaired cats breeding with shorthaired cats that were also brought to Norway with the Vikings around 1000 A.D.

Since they had trade routes with the Byzantium, it is possible this breed started with the Turkish Andorra cat. Many of the coat colors seen in these cats were rarely seen in other European domestic cats, but were common in the Turkish breed.

The cats were able to naturally adapt to their environment, growing a long thick coat to protect them against the very cold climates. The fur of the Norwegian Forest cat is long on top with a short thick coat underneath that helps keep them warm.

Their coats also help to shed water to keep them dry when it snows or rains. Their coats are long and flowing during the cold winter months, but as the weather gets warmer, they shed much of topcoat, leaving them with shorter, less dense fur for the summer months.

They are a strong, sturdy breed of cat with long legs and a bushy tail. These cats have strong claws, making them expert climbers and they love to be up in high places. They are definitely not a dainty cat as their average weight is between seven and 20 pounds.

Along with their sturdy stature and distinctive coats, the standard for the breed are all shades of green or gold, but pure white cats may have blue or odd colored eyes. The coats of this breed come in all patterns and colors.

The Norwegian Forest cat first caught the eye of cat lovers during a cat show in Germany during the late 1930s. Soon, war broke out in Europe and breeding cats became a very low priority by people just trying to survive one day at a time.

After World War II, their numbers rapidly declined and they were all but extinct by the 1970s. The Norwegian Forest Cat Club came to the rescue and initiated an official breeding program to save them. They also received a royal designation by King Olaf V when he was named as Norway's official cat during this time.

A cat lover in Norway, Carl-Fredik Nordane, took notice of the breed and decided to have it registered. His efforts helped the Norwegian Forest cat become registered with Europe's Fédération Internationale Féline, commonly known as FiFe.

By 1977, breeding began on an international level. In the same year, the breed was recognized as a "distinct pedigree" in Norway. A distinct pedigree is one that is recognized as a purebred cat breed.

While these cats are still very popular in Norway, Iceland, Sweden and France, they can be found in many different parts of the world. The first breeding pair of Norwegian Forest cats was introduced to the United States in 1979 as part of the international breeding program.

Along with FiFe, the "Wegie," as they have been nicknamed in the U.S., are also recognized by all major cat associations like the Cat Fanciers' Association (CFA), The International Cat Association (TICA), the American Association of Cat Enthusiasts (AACE) and the Governing Council of the Cat Fancy (GCCF), which is an association in the United Kingdom.

Chapter 1 - The Origins of the Norwegian Forest Cat

These large domestic cats are very intelligent and mild-mannered, getting along great with people and other animals. They adapt very well to any environment and they enjoy being around families and children. They are also ready to play, so they make an excellent addition to any family who wants to lavish attention on them.

Despite their long fur, the Norwegian Forest cat is low maintenance, so they do not have to be constantly groomed like some other longhaired cat breeds. They are generally in good health, with a life span that ranges from 14 to 16 years.

However, like many purebred animals, they are prone to breed specific diseases. Kidney and heart problems have been reported in the Norwegian Forest cat, as well as a problem with the glycogen branching enzyme (GBE1).

GBE1 is a storage form of glucose, which is a necessary component within the body of mammals, including humans, because glucose is the main source of energy.

Mutations in GBE1 can cause hypoglycemic collapse in kittens when they are born, although most kittens with this disorder are stillborn, and it can also cause an onset of juvenile neuromuscular degeneration caused by glycogen storage disease type IV, which is a hereditary metabolic disorder.

Fortunately, these disorders can be tested for prior to breeding and the Norwegian Forest cats ready to be adopted should be certified that they do not have these diseases.

If you are curious about the breed and want to see it in action, try to attend a cat show and watch it go through its routine. A cat show is a great place to get a look at different breeds of cats, talk to those who own them or breed them and maybe even get a chance to pet one.

This beautiful breed is sure to be found in many cat shows, but you can always check online to find one near you and check to see if a Norwegian Forest cat will be in attendance.

Chapter 2 - Adopting a Norwegian Forest Cat

Before you decide to add any cat into your home, you need to research breeds to make sure which one will be compatible with you and your family.

All too often, people get kittens or other pets with expectations that are never met and these animals end up being surrendered to an animal shelter or abandoned. To avoid problems with compatibility, it is best to read all you can on the specific breed of cat that you are thinking about adopting to see if you have the time to devote to your new family addition before you take one home.

If you do discover that the Norwegian Forest cat would be a good cat to bring into the family, the best place to adopt one is from a caring breeder at one of the many catteries found in the U.S. that specialize in this breed. A good way to find the nearest cattery is to go to the website for the "Fanciers Breeders Referral List," found at http://www.breedlist.com/ On their site, you can search for catteries by specific breed or by location.

Another good site to find general information about this cat breed and to find breeders is the Norwegian Forest Cat Fanciers' Association website at http://www.forestcats.net/ This association not only lists breeders in the United States, but it lists breeders around the world as well. All of the breeders on the page are members of the NFCFA, which is dedicated to the preservation and protection of not only this breed, but also all cats in general.

Even though the breed has been around for centuries, in the U.S., they are considered a relatively new breed, as they were not introduced into the country until 1979. As such, many cat fanciers may not have much, if any experience, with these cats other than having seen them in pictures or online. Like many purebred cats, it is rare that you will find a Norwegian Forest cat in an animal shelter or a pet store for adoption.

Chapter 2 - Adopting a Norwegian Forest Cat

There are many other general cat sites that list breeders by specific breed and location of the catteries who handle them. Some of these general sites include Breeding-Cats.com, http://www.breeding-cats.com/norwegian-forest-cat-breeders.html#United States, and the Cat Channel at http://www.catchannel.com/classifieds/listing-norwegian-forest-cat.aspx

For people who may not wish to adopt a kitten because they don't have time to care for the needs of a baby, there are organizations dedicated to finding homes for cats who had to be given up or who were abandoned, which includes some Norwegian Forest cats.

There is a specific website set up for rescuing this breed and they list cats available for adoption by location, whether in the U.S. or around the world. The site, the Norwegian Forest Cat Rescue, is located at http://norwegianforestcat.rescueme.org/ Animal organizations and individuals will list the cats they need to have adopted, usually with a photo and some brief information about the cat's personality.

The Norwegian Forest cat would make a nice addition to most homes as they like being around people and other pets. They like to climb and play, so it is a good idea to prepare for them by having a tall cat tree put into the area of your home designated for your cat.

Make sure that this area is someplace where the family will be as well because these cats like hanging out with their people and they will bond with other animals in the household, including the family dog, if given the chance.

If you do decide to get your new cat from a breeder, whether it is a Norwegian Forest cat or another breed, there are some questions and requests you may want to ask when you call or visit the cattery.

Are They Certified?

Find out if the kittens in the litter you are adopting from have been given a clean bill of health and find out if their parents have been certified as well.

Any breeder who claims that the "Wegie" has no genetic diseases should be dismissed from your consideration as that is not true. If a breeder is unable or unwilling to show certification or provide a health guarantee for their kittens, dismiss them as well.

Meet the Parents

If you are able to visit the cattery, ask to see the parents of the kitten you are thinking of adopting. As kittens can inherit personality traits from the parents, interacting with the Queen and the Tom is a good way to discover the kitten's potential temperament and visually examine them to see how healthy they look and determine if the cats seem to be from a good home.

Are the Kittens Socialized?

Socialization is very important for kittens and should start at about six weeks of age. When kittens are socialized, they are gradually introduced to the world around them in order to help them be comfortable in their surroundings. They should be handled and played with by people, including supervised children.

The kittens should be introduced to other cats, dogs and animals so they don't fear them. They should also be around noises such as the television, vacuum and other objects so they don't get scared when they hear these noises in their new homes.

Ask for a Tour

If you live near the cattery you are getting your Norwegian Forest cat from, ask for a tour of the facility or home. A reputable breeder will be glad to show you around and let you inspect the home where the kitten has been living. If the breeder will not let you see the facilities, then dismiss them from your consideration as they are probably hiding something.

Are their Shots Up-to-Date?

By the time you take your kitten home, they should have had most of their inoculations and have been dewormed. Ask to see their records on the kitten's visits to the vet and find out if the kitten has been declared healthy.

Find out if the breeder offers a health guarantee on their kittens and about any refunds in case you do end up with a sickly cat. While it is not an absolute guarantee that you will not get a sick cat, it does help weed out those who might be ill already.

Ask for Referrals

Most reputable catteries keep good records on their adopted kittens and they often stay in touch with the adopted homes so they can keep tabs on their cats. Ask for referrals to some of their customers and call to find out how they liked their adoption experience with the cattery.

Most breeders will have customers who are only too happy to be used as referrals. However, if the breeder refuses to give you referrals that can be a sign that you need to find a different cattery from which to adopt a kitten.

By asking questions and doing research online, you should be able to find a reputable breeder from which to adopt a Norwegian Forest kitten. You may also want to consider a retired cat as they are usually not very old and make good pets.

A retired cat is one that has been used for breeding, but is no longer bred either due to age or because the breeder only wanted to get one or two litters from the cat and has done so. An older cat is a great way to add a new pet to your family, especially if you don't have the time to take care of a kitten.

Chapter 3 - Bringing Your New Kitten Home

When it is time to introduce your new kitten to its forever home, you should be ready to properly care for your Norwegian Forest cat or Wegie. They are low-maintenance cats for the most part, but kittens always require more care than adult cats.

Properly caring for your new kitten includes knowing how to properly groom them, which foods they should, and should not, be fed, which shots they will need in the future. The breeder from which you adopted your kitten should be able to give you a detailed list of the shots your kitten has had and which ones they will need in the future.

Chapter 3 - Bringing Your New Kitten Home

Kittens should be fully weaned by the time they are eight weeks old, so they should be eating solid kitten food. While some breeders like to retain their kittens until they are about 16 weeks old, others will begin to adopt out kittens as soon as they get to nine weeks of age.

If you adopt your kitten from a breeder that waits until it has reached about four months ago, the kitten should have had its vaccinations against feline leukemia, the feline immunodeficiency virus, rabies and other disease known to attack kittens.

The last of these shots are administered around 14 to 18 weeks of age and they will only require a yearly booster once their vaccinations are done. They should have been dewormed and treated for fleas too.

Just as you would for a human baby, you should ready your home for a new kitten before you pick him or her up from the cattery. In order to be comfortable, there are some items you should pick out for your new kitten and have waiting for it when it gets home.

At the very minimum, you should have a litter box, litter, food and water bowls, along with food ready to go. Preferably, they should have a cat bed so they have a comfortable place to call their own and some toys to occupy their time.

If you have the room in your home, try to set up the cat supplies in an area that you can close off with a baby gate or some people will put a new kitten into a small playpen when they are not going to be home or at night with their toys and access to water. This helps keep the new kitten confined to their area in order to help them get comfortable in their new home and keeps them from discovering the nooks and crannies in which they can easily get lost.

If you've adopted your kitten from an experienced breeder, it has probably been well socialized so it won't be fearful of every new thing it comes across. However, that doesn't mean you won't have a shy kitten.

If your kitten seems shy or if it hasn't been socialized well and it may immediately hide from you when you get it home. If it does hide, don't be alarmed and don't force it to socialize with you, but allow the kitten to discover the new territory on its own and become acclimated.

Introduce your new kitten to its area, especially the litter box so it knows where to go potty. This should be within or close to their area, but away from their food and water supply. Cats don't want to eat near where they've defecated and you wouldn't either. Put some space between their restroom area and the feeding area, even if that means only feeding them in the kitchen. However, always have water nearby for when it gets thirsty.

Feeding them in the kitchen is a good way to start acquainting your kitten with the rest of the house as well.

Just as you would with a human baby, kittens should be kept on a feeding schedule. Although many people free feed their cats, which means leaving a bowl of dry food out for them all the time, for some cats this is a bad habit because it will only make them fat.

It is far better to feed your kitten at set times so they get used to their feeding schedule and not get used to having access to food 24 hours a day.

A kitten less than six months old should be fed three times a day. Once it has reached six months of age, you can cut back to feeding it twice a day until they have reached the age of nine months.

At that time, you can cut them back to once a day, but feeding them twice a day allows the kitten to keep its energy levels high and stay healthy. A Wegie is playful and likes to climb, so they need all the energy they can get.

When selecting a diet for your kitten, you have two options, dry and wet commercial foods or a raw food diet. If you select the raw food diet, feeding it raw egg yolks, chicken, liver and other raw meats, you will need to give her or him a calcium supplement until it is nine months old.

Dry foods for kittens are supplemented with calcium, so they do not need to be given any further dietary supplements. Once a cat has reached nine months of age, they can be switched to an adult diet.

Although clumping litter is okay to use for adult cats, you shouldn't buy it for your kitten's litter box. Curious kittens will sometimes eat litter and, if it is the clumping kind, it can get clumped together in its throat or stomach and kill the kitten. Buy a litter box with sides short enough for the kitten to be able to easily climb in and out, in addition, always make sure to keep it clean. If you notice your kitten is using the toilet outside of the litter box, it could mean that the litter box needs to be cleaned or the kitten cannot climb into the litter box.

When you go to work, your cat will quickly get bored if they don't have something to stimulate them. Buy soft toys your kitten can bat around and carry in their mouths. Many kittens will keep themselves entertained for hours if they have toys readily available.

Since Wegies like to climb, if you hope to keep your drapes or furniture claw free, invest in a tall cat tree. It will give them something to climb, a perch to sit or lay down on and it can sharpen its claws on the cat tree as well.

Buy toys that you can use to interact with your kitten too. Wegies quickly grow to love their human companions and they like to play with them as well as snuggle . Exercise is a good way for you to help expend some of the kitten's energy before bedtime so it will settle down to sleep and let you get some sleep as well.

Chapter 4 - Properly Grooming Your Norwegian Forest Cat

An important part of owning a Norwegian Forest cat, or any cat, is keeping them groomed. Not only is grooming essential to keep them looking beautiful, but it also helps ensure that they are healthy.

Even though Wegies have long fur, they do not require constant grooming to keep their coats looking their best. You can usually get by with brushing your Norwegian Forest cat once a week in the winter months, but when they start shedding in the spring, you will want to brush them more frequently to keep their fur from shedding all over your furniture and carpets.

Other essential grooming tasks include trimming their nails, checking their ears and brushing their teeth on a regular basis. All of these activities will help keep your Wegie healthier and, in some cases, help extend their lives. A Norwegian Forest cat has a coat of soft, thick fur as an adult, but they don't usually have a mature coat until they are at least two years of age and your kitten won't start developing its adult coat until it turns three months old.

Even though your kitten will have a sparse coat, you should begin to gently brush it in order to get it used to the grooming process. Use a brush or comb and gently brush out their coat at least once a week. The Wegie's coat can become tangled and matted if neglected, so it is good to start getting your kitten used to the process at an early age. This way they don't fight you when they need to be brushed.

Although their fur is water resistant, you may wish to get your kitten used to water baths when they are young. Some cats like water and the Norwegian Forest cat doesn't mind it, but you will want to introduce it to the concept of a water bath at a young age so it doesn't panic if it ever needs a bath. If a water bath is out of the question, try using a dry shampoo on their coat to help keep their coat clean.

Norwegian Forest cats also have tufted ears that need to be checked at least once a week. Check their ears for redness or a bad smell, which could indicate an ear infection. If the cat's ears are dirty, gently clean them with a cotton ball that is slightly dampened with an ear cleanser your veterinarian has recommended. Do not trim the hair from their ears as it helps to protect them from the cold winter weather. During the summer, your cat will have a sparser coat, fully tufted ears and a bushy tail leftover to show off.

As part of their grooming routine, your cat's nails should be trimmed once a week. Wegies love to climb and they need to have strong nails to help them get up to their favorite perch.

If a cat's nails are neglected, they can curl under and grow into the pad of their toes, like an ingrown toenail for humans, and cause them pain as they attempt to walk. If you start trimming your kitten's nails, they will get used to the process and it will make it easier to perform the task.

There are three styles of clippers to choose from for animals; a guillotine type clipper in which the tip of the nail is inserted into the head of the clipper and lopped off, a scissor cut style of clipper and a human toenail clipper. A human toenail clipper or the guillotine style work best for cats, but if your cat has long curls on its nails, you will need the scissor style to cut them off.

Fortunately, most cats have light colored or translucent claws, which make it easier to trim them. Their clear color makes it easier to see the quick of the cat's nails, which you need to avoid.

While the nails don't have nerve endings, the quick does and, if you accidentally cut into it, the experience will be painful for your cat and the quick can bleed profusely. The quick will appear as a pink stripe inside of the nail, about 2 millimeters from the tip of the nail.

A cat's toenails are retractable, so all you have to do in order to trim them is place their paw in your hand and gently press down on their toe with your fingertip and thumb. The nail should easily protract, allowing you to trim it. Clipping off the tip or the hook of the nail is sufficient and they can use the cat tree or a scratching post to help shorten their nails and keep them sharp.

Tooth decay and gum disease are problems for many cats, including the Norwegian Forest cat. This breed is susceptible to periodontal disease, so it is important that you check their gums and brush their teeth as part of your grooming routine. Start them off as young kittens so they can get used to having their teeth brushed on a regular basis and you may need to schedule occasional cleanings with your vet as well.

Plaque from food and bacteria builds up on cat's teeth just as it does on humans' and plaque-causing bacteria can sometimes get into their bloodstream. If it does, it can damage their internal organs and lead to death. It isn't uncommon for older cats to lose teeth to plaque build up, but if you brush their teeth regularly, they will get to keep their teeth longer.

Your veterinarian can show you what type of toothbrush to use and which dental products are safe for your cat. He or she can also show you how to properly brush your cat's teeth. Plaque builds up on the outside of their teeth, not the inside, so brushing their teeth is easy to do, it just require diligence and patience.

If you have young kittens, don't brush their milk teeth as they will fall out and permanent teeth will grow in to replace them. However, it is a good time to get the kittens used to having their teeth touched. Gently open their lips and carefully touch their teeth with your finger or a damp washcloth, rubbing very gently. Doing this will start getting them used to the brushing process and make it easier for them to adapt when it is time to brush their teeth.

Sometimes, no matter what you do, a cat just will not tolerate having their teeth brushed. If this is the case with your kitten or cat, your veterinarian can recommend an oral product to keep their teeth healthy. In addition, you can feed adult cats a dental formula dry food.

Check their eyes during your cat's grooming routine as well. Some time, cats get "sleep" in their eyes that needs to be gently wiped away. Using a cotton swab, gently wipe their eye, starting from the nose side outwards, to remove this gunk from their eyes. Be sure to use a clean swab for each eye to avoid passing an infection from one eye to another. If they have a discharge in their eye, wipe it away using the same method and call your vet if it lasts for more than two days.

A grooming routine will help keep your Norwegian Forest cat beautiful, healthy and happy for many years. As soon as you bring your kitten home, start their grooming routine to get them used to being brushed and handled. This will make grooming a less stressful time for your cat and it will help to keep you from being clawed or bit. A win-win for both you and your cat companion.

Chapter 5 - Health Issues Found in the Norwegian Forest Cat Breed

There are many medical issues that cats can suffer from that are the result of their heredity. Although the Norwegian Forest cat is a sturdy breed and has been alive for centuries, it does suffer from its share of ailments. Some of the medical problems they have are unique to the breed, but there are diseases that other cat breeds can suffer from as well. The medical issues that the Wegie is known to suffer from include:

Hypertrophic cardiomyopathy

Glycogen storage disease type IV

Hip dysplasia

Retinal Dysplasia

Hypertrophic Cardiomyopathy

This heart disease is the most common cardiac problem in cats and it is also the most common cause of spontaneous death in indoor adult cats.

The walls of the heart, specifically the ventricles, thicken or hypertrophy and make it harder for the cat's heart to function properly. The muscle fiber in the heart is replaced by connective tissue, scar tissue, but instead of making the heart pump harder, in cats, this condition weakens the heart because the heart chambers are reduced in size.

It is hard to detect early signs of HCM because the symptoms can be vague, but an increased heart rate and a heart murmur are some of the common signs of this disease. A cat may also have an increased respiration rate, they may have a decreased appetite and you may notice it has lost weight.

Their loss of appetite or lethargy may go undetected because cats are intelligent and recognize their limitations when they are ill and decrease their activity accordingly. The first real sign of HCM is often sudden death of the cat.

As the left ventricle loses its ability to function properly, some cats may start showing symptoms such as pulmonary edema, which means that fluid is filling the lungs. The signs of this are rapid breathing, wheezing, lethargy, a dry cough and they may be unable to play.

Pleural effusion is also a symptom that may appear and it means the fluid is filling the sac that wraps around the lungs. This symptom constricts the lungs and the cat will have breathing problems with this symptom too.

Chapter 5 - Health Issues Found in the Norwegian Forest Cat Breed

An echocardiogram is often used to diagnosis this condition and, if caught soon enough, your veterinarian may prescribe drugs that relax the heart and increase its ability to pump blood. Most of the drugs that treat heart conditions in humans may be used in small animals, but the drugs your vet will prescribe depend on how ill the cat is and if they have any complications, such as an arrhythmia.

The drugs he or she prescribes may include calcium channel blockers, diuretics, beta-blockers and ACE inhibitors. They may prescribe aspirin as well. Only give your cat aspirin if your veterinarian has prescribed it. Improper dosing can kill a cat.

Hypertrophic cardiomyopathy usually affects cats from ages one to five years of age. However, it has been diagnosed in kittens as young as three months old and in cats as old as 10.

Dismiss breeders from your consideration if they claim to have HCM-free lines of Norwegian Forest cats because no one can guarantee that the disease will never develop in a cat. Testing can be done to screen Wegies for the disease and any cat that tests positive shouldn't be bred.

Glycogen Storage Disease Type IV

This disease is an inherited deficiency in the glycogen branching enzyme, GBE1, that is required to properly process glycogen. Glycogen is a form of glucose that is used for energy in a cat's body. Similarly, humans also process glucose from the foods they eat and it supplies fuel for their bodies as well. The disease can cause an altered form of glycogen to gather on the nerves and muscles in the cat's body.

Sometimes this disease will affect kittens right at birth and they will usually be stillborn or they may die shortly after birth. This manifestation of the disease is called perinatal hypoglycemic collapse. It is thought that the disease prevents the kittens from receiving the energy they need to survive.

Another manifestation is called late-juvenile-onset neuromuscular degeneration and it becomes apparent in the kitten by the time it is four or five months old. A kitten that develops this disease may run an intermittent fever, have tremors and be unable to control its muscle movements. Its growth then stops and it will develop severe muscle weakness, contractions, atrophy and it will be unable to care for itself, eat and use its limbs, especially the back legs. The disease leads to cardiac failure, coma and eventually death before the age of 15 months. Usually, these cats are put to sleep so they won't suffer.

Fortunately, DNA can be used to test cats to see if they are carriers of the disease. As it is an autosomal recessive trait in this breed, kittens are rarely born with the disease because both parents have to be carriers of the disease in order to pass it on to their offspring. Breeders should get DNA tests for their Wegies and if they are found to be carriers of this disease, they should be withdrawn from the breeding program.

Hip Dysplasia

Although it is usually associated with dogs, hip dysplasia can also affect cat breeds. It is a hereditary defect in cat breeds like the Norwegian Forest cat and it is characterized by the socket joint in the pelvis being too shallow. When the sockets are too shallow, the ball of the hip doesn't fit as it should and the bones rub together, causing the cartilage to degenerate. When the cartilage wears away, the cat is left with a bone on bone joint, which causes the cat pain when it moves.

The body cannot grow more cartilage and when it tries to fix the problem, more bone is produced, making the problem worse. Cats that have hip dysplasia may not show signs of pain, especially if the problem is minor. Their activities may curtail, they may not jump any more or they may very carefully. If they have a bad case of this disease, they may walk with an odd gait and if you try to touch the hip area, they may seem to be in pain. If this happens, they will need to be taken to their vet for an examination. The condition is detected with x-rays and, if the case is severe, the cat may need to have hip replacement surgery.

Cats that are being considered for breeding should be screened for hip dysplasia. After they are examined and x-rayed, the cat's hip dysplasia is graded by the severity of the disease, if it is detected. For cats with moderate to severely affected hips, they should be taken out of the breeding program since it is a hereditary condition that can be passed onto their offspring.

Retinal Dysplasia

This condition causes a malformation of the eyes' retina. In minor cases of the disease, it may cause small blind spots in the affected cat's vision that may not be noticeable to the owner or even the cat. Severe cases may cause large malformations that can cause some loss of vision or blindness. The malformations may appear as folds or rosettes on the kitten's eyes.

Retinal Dysplasia is caused in utero or soon after kittens have been born. Although the disease can be hereditary, it is usually caused by a virus like the feline leukemia virus or feline panleukopenia. There is no known treatment at this time.

Despite these conditions, the Norwegian Forest cat is known for its sturdiness and its longevity. When you adopt your Wegie from a breeder, ask to see a medical clearance and, if one cannot be produced, consider finding another breeder.

A reputable breeder should be able to produce all veterinary records for their kittens immediately upon request, unless they are hiding something. Also, ask about guarantees for the kitten if a serious illness is detected.

The best way to ensure your cat's health is to feed him or her a healthy diet so they maintain a healthy weight. A healthy weight for a Wegie can be between seven and 20 pounds.

This will help keep pressure off their joints so they won't wear down as fast as they would in a heavier cat. Along with a healthy diet, help your cat to remain active by playing with him or her and take it to the vet for regular check-ups.

Chapter 6 - How to Find a Good Vet for Your Cat

Your cat's veterinarian will be your partner in helping you keep your cat healthy and happy, so it is important to find a vet that you can trust to properly treat your cat. A vet not only needs to be good with animals, but they should also be people oriented in order to instruct and help pet owners properly care for their furry companions.

You shouldn't wait until you have a medical emergency to find a vet; you should choose your vet before you bring the new family addition home.

A good way to find a veterinarian is to ask the pet lovers in your life for vet recommendations. If your family, friends and coworkers have a vet they like, they will be glad to give you a referral and, if they have had a bad experience with a vet, you will also quickly hear about their experience.

It is a good way to either quickly eliminate vets from consideration for your Norwegian Forest kitten or find those you will need to interview for your cat's care.

In most larger communities, there are veterinarians that specialize in cat care. Although you don't necessarily need to take your cat to a vet who specializes in cat care, it could be a better option since you are bringing home a purebred cat.

Cat veterinarians have been trained how to handle cats and educated about the various diseases that affect them. If you happen to live in an area with cat specialists available to you, consider interviewing them to handle for your cat's care.

The veterinarian is only one member of a team that will be responsible for your cat's medical care. Usually in the vet's office, there will be technicians, vet assistants, caretakers and other support staff that will also be responsible for part of your cat's care. When you go interview the veterinarian, you should also evaluate the support staff's ability to handle your cat in a caring, competent manner.

Although it shouldn't be your first or only consideration for selecting a vet, ask about their fee schedule for check-ups, treatment and emergency care so you can compare them with the other veterinarians you are considering.

Find out if they offer senior or multiple pet discounts, if applicable to your situation. Check to see how far of a drive the vet's office is from your home to determine how long it would take to get there in an emergency. Driving a few miles out of your way or paying a slightly higher free may be well worth the effort in order to find a great vet for your Wegie.

Conduct an online search for cat hospitals and other veterinarians as well. Most businesses today have websites to promote their services and you can find contact information, hours of operation, information about their services and sometimes there is staff information too. The Internet is a great resource when you are looking for a veterinarian or general information about Norwegian Forest cats.

When you have a list of veterinarians to interview to become your cat's doctor, check to see if they have accreditation with the American Animal Hospital Association. The accreditation process for the AAHA is voluntary and it shows that the vets who are accredited meet the association's standards for the quality care of animals and that their facility and equipment have met the AAHA's standards as well.

Should you ever need to take your cat to a specialist, find out if they have been board certified. Certification requires an additional two to four years of study, depending on their area of expertise, and they also have to pass a rigorous examination in order to finalize their certification.

If the specialist is not board certified, dismiss them from consideration for your pet's care, if you have a choice. Depending on the specialty, you may have to take your cat there any way if there isn't another specialist in your area.

Once you have your final list of veterinarians that you are considering, schedule an appointment to meet them and tour their facility. Meeting with the vet will let you evaluate their ability to discuss medical matters with you and help you start building a rapport with them.

During the tour, meet with members of the support staff and try to evaluate their ability to talk with pet owners and handle pets as well. Most vets will be happy to give your a tour of their offices and pet care areas and if they are reluctant, be wary because that could be a sign that they are hiding something from their clients.

Take a list of questions that you may have with you so you don't forget to ask them. Find out if the vet has had any experience treating a Norwegian Forest cat and, if they have, that will be a big plus in their favor as these cats are not that common in the United States.

Be sure to ask questions about the facility's policies and find out the vet's philosophy about treating pets, euthanasia and other concerns that you have.

Making a visual inspection of the facility during the tour will give you a lot of good information. It will allow you to observe its cleanliness, how well organized it is kept and whether it looks comfortable for the pets being treated. If the facility has dog and cat patients, find out if the cages are kept separate or if they are kept in the same room.

If you see something you don't like about the facility, don't be afraid to ask questions about it.

Find out how much of their testing is done in-house and whether you would need to take your pet to a specialist to have an EKG, x-ray, ultrasound or other testing done on your cat.

Also, find out if they have lab facilities onsite to analyze blood work or if it is sent to an outside lab. If it is sent out to a lab, that could delay test results, which could be crucial if your cat is seriously ill. Find out if they are available for emergency care and which emergency services they offer.

After you've selected the veterinarian you intend on bringing your cat to for care, play your part in the team effort to keep your cat healthy. Schedule an appointment for your new kitten so the vet can start building a rapport with both you and your new family member. By taking your cat to the vet for regular check-ups, it allows the vet to get to know your cat so he or she can better treat it when your cat is sick.

Observing your cat will help you get to know their normal routine and behaviors. This will make it easier to detect when your cat isn't feeling well or has been injured. Don't wait until your cat gets worse to call the vet, call their office as soon as you notice something wrong with your cat. Having your cat tested right away can be essential in being able to successfully treat them. Time is of the essence when a cat is ill and it is important that treatment is started right away. Waiting could be fatal for them in many cases.

Whenever you do transport your cat to the vet, take him or her in a cat carrier. Many cats do not like to travel in a car, even for just a few blocks and using a cat carrier will help protect both them and you. Bring them home in a cat carrier so it can start getting used to being in the carrier when you need to use it. Some cats will quickly take to it and even be curious enough when you open it to voluntarily walk into it and investigate the carrier.

Between the time you pick out your kitten and get to take him or her home, you should have ample opportunity to research, interview and decide whom you will use as your cat's veterinarian. Along with taking your cat in for regular check-ups and shots, you should be a caring, responsible pet owner whenever you visit the vet's office.

Keep control of your cat, ask questions and get to know the staff taking car of your furry family member. Developing a good relationship with your vet and the staff will help in keeping your cat healthy throughout its life.

Chapter 7 - The Personality of the Norwegian Forest Cat

Although personalities can vary from one cat to another, even within the same litter, there are personality traits that purebred cats are well known to possess. The Norwegian Forest cat is known as a friendly cat with a high intelligence level and a curious, alert gaze.

Their expression is due in part to their well-proportioned triangular head featuring expressive, almond-shaped eyes and straight nose with a firm chin. However, they don't just look smart, but the Wegie is a very smart breed.

The Wegie is an adaptable breed and they usually get along with any human or animal they encounter. It isn't unusual for them to develop a bond with their new family's dog, if there is one in the house. Their curious, courageous nature allows them to get along well with other cats and children as well.

The Norwegian Forest cat will usually form a strong bond with its owner or one member of their new family, but even though they will get along well with the other members in the family, most of their attention will be lavished on one person.

Some Wegies are very content to be lap cats, but not all of them are suited for that position. However, that doesn't mean they won't interact with you. Wegies love attention and they will seek it out when they want your focus to be on them.

They will demand that you pet or scratch them under the chin by bumping your hand or they may exchange head bumps with you, which is their way of saying they trust you.

This breed is people oriented, so they usually want to hang out with their special person. When you set up their cat tree or a perch, put it where you and/or your family are most of the time. They want to be with their family as much as possible.

Most Wegies will take to following their person around the house. If you are cleaning the house, you may notice them following in your footsteps as your go from room to room.

While they are usually laid back cats, if you bring out a favorite toy, you will have all of your Wegie's attention. Most Norwegian Forest cats give 110% when it is playtime and you will see a full display of their hunter instincts when they stalk their "prey," pounce on it and try to capture it.

Just before they launch their attack, they will coil their bodies and swish their tails, signaling their intentions. Built with muscular legs, they are good jumpers and climbers, so they know no limits when it comes to hunting their "prey."

Once they have their "prey," don't be surprised if you see your Wegie toss it into the air and stalk it all over it again. They can keep themselves entertained for several minutes at a time when they play with their favorite toys.

When you pick up the supplies for your new kitten, be sure to include several soft toys that are easy for them to carry around. Include a catnip toy or two for some serious fun and entertainment.

Interactive play is important as well, so include wand toys that will allow you to join in the fun with your cat. Spots of light will also capture their undivided attention; and even if it disappears, your Wegie won't easily give up on the game.

He or she is more apt to wait for the light to reappear so the game can resume than he or she is to completely abandon it, even if they have to wait for an hour or more. They are a patient breed, but more importantly, they are always ready to play a fun game.

While they are not very vocal cats, the breed does have a variety of trills and chirps that sound almost bird-like. If you know your cat, you will be able to distinguish its mood by the sounds he or she makes. Whether it is a soft meow or playful "chirps," they will express themselves to you on occasion.

Since they do get along with other pets, people and they adapt very well, the Norwegian Forest cat will make a great addition to any family. They are intelligent creatures with more than enough affection for their human family and their other pet friends as well.

Chapter 8 - Cat Misbehaviors and Causes

Although the Norwegian Forest cat is mild mannered most of the time, there are medical issues and circumstances that can cause behavior problems in even the most even-tempered breed.

There can be many causes for bad cat behaviors, including a rough beginning to their life, neglect, it can be a sign of aging, a dietary deficiency or it could be a sign that they are bored because they are left alone too much.

If your normally laid back cat suddenly develops behavior problems, make an appointment with your cat's veterinarian to eliminate physical ailments that might be causing the problems. By eliminating a physical reason for their behavior, you can concentrate on retraining your cat in order to correct the problems they are having. Retraining cats isn't difficult and the Wegie's intelligence helps to make it even easier to accomplish.Some common cat behavior problems include:

Soiling outside the litter box.

Destructive chewing or scratching.

Excessive vocalization.

Aggressiveness

Jumping where they are not allowed.

It is important to observe and get to know your cat's traits so you can notice changes in their behavior right away. If it is due to a medical condition, then you can get them help as soon as you are aware of the problem. The sooner you get them treated the better, as some illnesses can quickly prove fatal to cats.

Some of these behaviors will develop as a cat gets older, as they can suffer from senility much like humans. If you adopt an older cat, they may have behaviors that caused their previous owners to give them up, but by retraining them, along with patience and love, you can correct their bad behaviors.

Soiling Outside the Litter Box

Urinating or defecating outside of the litter box is the number one reason that many cats are surrendered to animal shelters and it may be one of the easiest problems to solve.

If your cat suddenly starts to eliminate outside of his or her litter box, you should try cleaning it out more often. Cats will refuse to use a dirty litter box and start eliminating nearby it if they deem it too smelly or unclean. Cats have a great sense of smell and if they think their box isn't clean enough, they may eliminate next to their litter box.

If the litter box is frequently cleaned, there could be a medical reason that they are choosing to eliminate outside of their litter box. A urinary tract infection may cause them to urinate outside of the litter box because they cannot make it there in time. If they have hemorrhoids or if they are constipated, they may defecate somewhere other than their box. If you notice these problems despite having a clean litter box, make an appointment with the vet to have your cat examined for medical issues.

Spraying Urine

Cats can be very territorial, especially with other cats they do not like, and they will mark their territory outdoors by spraying urine on it. However, if they are spraying indoors, it could be that they are marking their territory or it could be a sign of stress. Although Norwegian Forest cats are very adaptable, cats don't always respond well to changes. Cats can be stressed by the addition of a new pet or baby to their home and moving to another house could stress them out, especially if the cat had previously been surrendered to a shelter. An illness of a pet or human family member can also cause them stress.

If there have been recent changes in your household and your cat starts spraying, try to reassure him or her by lavishing your cat with extra attention. Once they know that everything is back to normal, the behavior should stop. You will also need to eliminate the urine odor by using an enzymatic cleaning product. These products neutralize the bacteria that cause the odors to help eliminate them. If the odor isn't dealt with, your cat will keep returning to the same spot and continue to spray.

Destructive Chewing

There can be several causes for destructive chewing and you should be concerned by the behavior. Some of the items your cat chooses to chew on could be harmful for them or they may choose something that you value to gnaw. Some of the common reasons for excessive chewing are teething in kittens, boredom, curiosity or it could be a sign of a diet deficiency.

To help end destructive chewing, make sure you are feeding your cat a healthy, balanced diet in order for them to remain healthy and active. If your kitten is teething, give them a large straw to chew on, they will also find it fun to bat around and carry from place to place. Discourage chewing on cords, which can be very tempting for cats, and houseplants, as many of those are poisonous to cats. Use something to make them taste bad, such as apple bitter or gently spraying them from a water bottle will discourage most bad behaviors

Destructive Scratching

Supplying your cat with plenty of scratching surfaces doesn't mean they will leave your furniture and carpets alone, although it will help to reduce the odds of them using those surfaces for their primarily scratching needs. Scratching acts as exercise for your cat, helping them relieve stress and it keeps their claws maintained. Having scratching pads, scratching posts or even a large log will help to keep your cat away from your furniture and rugs.

If they do start scratching on your furniture or carpets, discourage their behavior with a short squirt of water from a spray bottle, trim their nails, or if the situation warrants, use nail caps.

Declawing a cat should never be considered, as that is like cutting off their fingers. A cat uses their nails to grip when they climb and to pull things to them.

Excessive Vocalization

Norwegian Forest cats are not known for meowing too much, although they will "talk" to you at times. They seek attention by butting your hand or rubbing against your leg, but they will chirp in excitement or purr in contentment when they are snuggling with you. However, some people do have cats that loudly cry or meow and if your Wegie does this, it could be cause for concern.

Excessive vocalization can be a sign of a physical or an emotional issue, although it is normal behavior for some cat breeds or individual cats. As cats age, they may "howl" at night as if they are lost and it can be caused when cats are going deaf or by senility in some senior cats. If your Wegie starts loudly meowing, especially at night, call your vet to have him or her evaluated.

Aggressiveness

Even the most mild-mannered cat can turn aggressive in certain situations and people unwittingly encourage their aggression by giving into them when they are hissed or swatted. Aggression can be brought on by physical discomfort, illness or sometimes a situation will trigger aggression in a cat.

If they are in pain, if they are resting and don't wish to be bothered, if they are protecting their territory or offspring or when forced into prolonged eye contact, they can turn aggressive.

Some health problems like hyperthyroidism or hyperesthesia syndrome, which is a neurological disorder that can cause seizures, can cause them to become aggressive. If you haven't added a new cat to your household, if they are not protecting themselves or their territory and they turn aggressive, contact your veterinarian to have your cat evaluated for medical conditions that could be causing the problem.

Jumping Where They Shouldn't

Most Wegies like to climb up as high as they can or jump up on high perches to hang out and relax, but there are places you may not want your cat to be.

If they jump on your kitchen counters, the top of a curio cabinet or up into your pantry, they could make a mess by knocking over valuables or get into food they shouldn't be eating. There are many ways to discourage this behavior and teach them not to go where they are not wanted.

If a simple and firm "no!" doesn't work, consider squirting them with a small amount of water or using sticky paper in the places they like to perch to discourage them. Most cats do not like water and they will not appreciate having sticky paper on their paws. Aluminum foil is a good option if you don't wish to use sticky paper. This should help discourage them from jumping where you don't want them to be.

Before trying other options, first eliminate medical causes for your cat's bad behavior if he or she suddenly develops any of these issues. If your Wegie starts behaving out of character, make an appointment with your vet to have them examined.

Catching a medical condition early will allow your cat to be treated and fully recover from any health problems they may have developed. Along with medical conditions, sometimes a cat's misbehaviors are caused by depression or other psychological issues and your vet should be able to diagnose and treat those problems as well.

Chapter 9 - Kitty Psychology: Helping Your Cat Deal with Shyness or Fear

Along with medical conditions, cats can end up with behavioral issues as a result of stress, anxiety and depression. They may also display OCD type behaviors caused by these problems.

Chapter 9 - Kitty Psychology: Helping Your Cat Deal with Shyness or Fear

It is important to know your cat's normal routines and behaviors so you can quickly spot problems when they first occur. If you know what to look for, you can help your cat either by soothing them or by having them treated by their veterinarian. "Bad" behavior often has a medical cause, such as an illness and the quicker the problem is found, the more likely it is for it to be treated successfully.

Even though the Norwegian Forest cat adapts well to most situations they are in, not every cat has the same personality. It isn't uncommon for some cats to be a little shy or standoffish, especially when thrust into a new environment.

If it is possible to do so, put your new family member into an area that you can close off with a baby gate so they can still see out into the rest of their new home. It will help them acclimate better to their new surroundings. In addition, you need to also interact with him or her as it will also help make their transition a smoother one.

Sometimes fear is mistaken for shyness because they can have the same root causes and the behaviors are almost the same. Fortunately, by being patient, you can help your new furry family member overcome their fear. Let the cat set his or her own pace because otherwise they may feel cornered

and resort to fighting with you or other animals in the
household.

Shyness or fear are not personality traits they have to be
stuck with for the rest of their lives, especially if a medical
condition is the underlying cause of their behavior.

Whenever you introduce a new cat into your home,
regardless if you adopted it from a shelter or a breeder, you
should make an appointment with the veterinarian you
have chosen for your cat's care and have them examined.
This allows any underlying medical issues to be discovered
and quickly treated.

Even though you may have papers showing that your
Wedgie has a clean bill of health, a check-up should still be
performed. It is also a good way to introduce the vet to
your cat.

Poor socialization is often another reason that a cat will
display signs of fear or shyness. A kitten should be
socialized with other cats, animals and humans starting at
about six weeks old. However, if they were removed from
their mother's care at a young age, they may not have been
fully socialized.

Chapter 9 - Kitty Psychology: Helping Your Cat Deal with Shyness or Fear

A kitten should stay with its mother for at least eight weeks, although 12 weeks is better and they are usually fully socialized by that age.

Changes in the cat's environment can cause them to be scared or shy as well. Humans even get shy when they are introduced to a new environment, such as a new school or starting a new job, so it understandable that a cat moving into a new home may experience bouts of shyness or fear.

Don't be surprised if your new addition hides away for a few days until they are adjusted to their new environment. Some cats have been known to stay hidden up to two weeks.

Patience is the key in helping your new cat deal with its shyness. Gently pet him or her while speaking in a soothing voice to try to reassure the cat. Let them explore their new surroundings on their own, without forcing the issue. Wegies easily adapt to new environments and if he or she is allowed to explore their new home on their terms, they will quickly get used to it.

Be sure they always have access to fresh water and a clean litter box. Put them on a feeding schedule and leave toys out so they can entertain themselves. As they get comfortable, they will begin to venture out further to explore their new surroundings and make themselves at home.

Some of the same causes of shyness will also trigger fear in some cats and a scared cat can sometimes react aggressively to humans and/or other animals. When you are trying to deal with a cat that is showing signs of fear, don't stare at him or her directly in the eyes. This is a sign of aggression for cats and it will trigger a "flight" or "fight" response. Most of the time, the cat will try to flee, unless it feels trapped and then it will start hissing, biting and clawing at you.

If you have other pets in your home, you need to introduce your new cat to your other pets gradually. Using a baby gate to block their access to the others will come in handy, especially if the cat is too small to leap or climb over the gate. The gate will allow them to see the other pets and get acquainted with them while keeping everyone safe.

Loud noises and environmental disasters may also trigger fear in cats. While the loud noises can be easily dealt with, an unexpected disaster can be problematic.

You will usually be aware of loud noises in your neighborhood and when they are scheduled to occur, such as construction, Fourth of July or New Year's Eve fireworks. This will allow you to put your cat some place where they feel safe and where they can't hear any loud sounds.

If you live in an area that has tornadoes, hurricanes, fires or where other natural disasters may occur, be prepared with an evacuation kit for your Wegie. The kit should include a cat carrier, enough food and water to last three to four days, a litter box, litter, something to calm them down when they are stressed and a favored toy or two. If you are prepared, it will be easier to deal with their fears and when you get back home, you can begin to soothe your cat's anxiety.

Fear and shyness are not the only psychological problems that can affect cats. They may also have problems with depression, OCD behaviors and stress. However, shyness and fear are two of the most common behaviors found in cats, even for breeds that normally have pleasant temperaments, such as the Norwegian Forest cat. If you are patient with a shy or scared cat and show them love, they will normally overcome their shyness or fear.

Chapter 10 - Kitty Psychology: Odd Cat Behaviors

Every cat has their moments when their behavior seems odd or when they seem to become manic for no reason at all. They may dash around the house, bounce off furniture or skitter across the floor in a frenzy. Usually this frisky behavior is a sign of playfulness, but they may also be demonstrating OCD behaviors. If you are familiar with their normal routines and behaviors, you will be able to easily interpret their actions and get them help, if it is warranted.

By now, you should be familiar with signs of shyness or fear in your cat, especially after reading the previous chapter. You should also begin to understand why your cat might be showing signs of stress or anxiety and you should also have a better understanding of how to start alleviating your cat's fears and shyness with patience, love and understanding.

There are many odd behaviors that your cat may start to exhibit if they are feeling stressed or anxious. Often times, these behaviors will be interpreted as OCD behaviors. OCD, or Obsessive Compulsive Disorder, is a behavioral disorder in which your cat may perform exaggerated, repetitive behaviors for seemingly no reason. Some cat OCD behaviors include:

Excessive Grooming

Compulsive Pacing

Sucking and/or Fabric Chewing

Excessive Grooming

Grooming or licking themselves excessively is usually a stress response in cats, but there could be a medical issue at the root of it as well. If you're familiar with cat behaviors, you know that cats will groom themselves when they are anxious or if they've committed a faux pas, such as falling off a piece of furniture while asleep. Some of the medical causes for over-grooming should be investigated before assuming it is a psychological or behavioral problem. Have your cat's vet check for fleas, allergies or fungal infections and have them treated accordingly.

Over-grooming may be a symptom of psychogenic alopecia. This problem will cause your cat to lick or groom itself to the point of baldness in some spots. If there is no underlying medical cause for this behavior, over-grooming is a sign of stress. Licking or grooming is a soothing behavior for cats and researchers have found that it releases endorphins in their brain. It can give a cat pleasure and act as a pain reliever. Your veterinarian will need to diagnose psychogenic alopecia when you have your cat examined.

You can help to soothe your cat and reduce their stress in many ways. You can cuddle and pet it while speaking to it in a soft voice or you can engage him or her in an activity, such as playing with a wand toy. If the problem is bad enough and it cannot be resolved by other means, your vet may put your cat on anti-anxiety medication.

Compulsive Pacing

Sometimes a cat that is stressed or anxious will pace back and forth or circle around for seemingly no reason. If this OCD behavior is accompanied by excessive grooming or fabric chewing, it may be trying to release endorphins so they feel more at ease. There are many triggers for this behavior, including moving into a new home, a new pet in the house or being adopted by new owners. Pacing or circling is their attempt to relieve the stress they are feeling.

They may also participate in this behavior if they perceive a threat or if they are bored. The threat may be a loud sound they are unfamiliar with or seeing another cat outside the window. The threat will provoke the "fight" or "flight" response, which energizes their body, and pacing or circling helps to release some of the energy. Cats that are confined to a small area will often pace or circle because they are bored and need to be active to escape the boredom.

Soothing your cat and spending time petting and/or cuddling with them with help alleviate some of their anxiety. If they seem stressed because of a threat, try to remove that threat or block their view to the outside so they think the threat is over. If you have to leave your cat confined while you are at work, put their favorite toys.in the room or crate where you keep them so they can entertain themselves until you get home.

Sucking and/or Fabric Chewing

Another behavior an anxious kitty may engage in is sucking or fabric chewing. Sometime it is caused when a kitten has been taken away from its mother at an early age. When they are in need of comfort, the cat will knead a blanket, or a cloth that is made from a texture they like and find soothing, and suck or chew on it similar to their actions as a kitten sucking at its mother's teat. A kitten's first source of comfort was feeding time and, if they were not properly socialized, they may resort back to it, even as.an adult cat.

The sucking could be directed at another object, their paws or even on your finger in an effort to seek out comfort. Fabric sucking or chewing isn't usually a cause for concern and it can be a good bonding experience for you and your cat. Make sure they are not ingesting the fabric they are sucking or chewing on and help sooth them by gently stroking them while speaking to them in a soft voice.

There are many cat behaviors that are playful as your cat makes an effort to try to communicate with you. Some of their antics may include:

Bunting

Butt Presentation

Cat Blinks

Covering Food

Face Sniffing

Laying on Your Things

Bunting

Bunting, head butting, or allorubbing serve two purposes for cats. First, they are leaving their scent on your when they rub against you or bump foreheads with you. Secondly, they are offering you an affectionate show of trust. Cats have scent glands on many parts of they bodies including under their chins, around their ears, the corners of their mouth, along their temples and tail.

At times your cat will head butt you or they may rub their head against your head, hands or rub their side against your leg. Usually, they are just leaving their scent on you, staking their claim in a way, but if they head butt you when their eyes are open, they are giving you a sign of trust. They usually only perform this behavior with other cats that they know are friendly.

Butt Presentation

Don't be offended if your cat turns around when you are petting him or her and seems to show you their butt. He or she is actually paying you a compliment and giving you an enthusiastic greeting. They will present their butts to other cats that they are well acquainted with and they trust. Cats often smell each other as a greeting. They will smell around the head and neck, then move down to the flanks and finally greet each other with a sniff on the rear. If their tail is raised while displaying their butt, they are signaling to the other cat that they are not a threat.

Cat Blinks

If you've ever noticed a cat seemingly winking or flirting with you by half-closing their eyes, that is exactly what they may be doing. The eye blink is a cat's version of a kiss. This behavior is usually done with other friendly cats and with the people they love. Their intentions with other cats, and even to humans, are communicated with their eyes.

A hard stare at another cat is an aggressive posture and it is their way of trying to intimidate them. The cat blink or cat kiss is a non-threatening gesture and it shows good intentions. They will usually repeat the blink if it is done to them, so the next time you have your cat's attention, open your eyes wide, blink slowly at them and you will probably get a kiss in return.

Covering Food

If you notice your cat attempting to cover their food or scratching around it, they may be trying to tell you that they don't like your food selection or they may like it so much that they want to save some for a snack. Feral cats have been observed covering food to find later when they are hungry. However, if you're trying a new food and your cat acts as if it is trying to cover it up, they are probably telling you that they don't like the food.

Face Sniffing

Norwegian Forest cats are curious creatures and their curiosity will often extend to their humans. They may sniff your face while you are cuddling them, which may be a greeting because they will greet friendly cats with a sniff about the head and neck. Your cat may also sniff your face, breath and overall scent because they love how you smell. He or she will love the attention you give it, as well as your warmth. If you don't mind it, let your cat smell you as much as they like as it will help you two bond.

Laying on Your Things

Have you ever been reading a book or the newspaper and have your cat plop itself down in the middle of it? Do they seem fascinated when you use your computer and try to lie on your keyboard? This is an attention seeking behavior, but it is also the way your cat is trying to tell you it just wants to be close to you. When you're doing something that relaxes you, being near you will relax your cat as well and make them feel more secure. Don't shoo him or her away when it happens, but give them a moment of your time and perhaps a cuddle.

Learning these behaviors and, the many others your cat may engage in, will help you better understand your cat. It will also help you better communicate with him or her. Do some further research online about cat behaviors to learn more about them.

Chapter 11 - Are You Ready to Adopt a Cat?

Although cats have a reputation for being very independent and standoffish, some breeds, such as the

Norwegian Forest cat, are people oriented and like being around their humans. They crave attention and will let you know so by bumping against your hand, jumping on your lap or following you from room to room. Cats need you to play, snuggle and care for them, especially a social breed like the Wegie.

Before adopting a cat, you should consider if you have the time it takes to properly care for one. While kittens are cute and cuddly, they do need attention and more care than an older cat.

If you don't have the time to invest into cat care, especially kitten care, you shouldn't adopt a cat. However, it doesn't take a large investment of time to properly take care of a cat and adopting a more mature cat may be a better option for you.

All too often, people will make a spur of the moment decision to adopt an animal and when it misbehaves or does something the owner doesn't like, they are surrendered to a shelter. To avoid that situation, do some research about cats to decide if you have the time and the resources to properly care for a cat, especially one that wants your attention like a Wegie. You should also consider whether you can financially afford to adopt a cat.

While it doesn't take a large investment of money to care for a pet, if you do want a purebred cat like a Norwegian Forest cat, you will pay significantly more to adopt one than you would an average housecat from a shelter. For a Wegie, expect to pay between $300 to $800 for one, depending on their age, the breeder and the cat's bloodlines.

Along with the costs associated for adopting your cat, you will need to buy food, litter and other supplies on a continual basis. They need a place to sleep, if you don't want them in your bed, a cat tree for climbing, a litter box, toys, a cat carrier, bowls for food and water, plus scratching posts at the minimum. Expect to pay about $50 or $60 per month on necessities, never mind the extras you may wish to splurge on for your cat.

As you will also have veterinary bills to pay for your cat, you should consider opening a small savings account dedicated to your cat to help pay for their bills. You never know when it may need to be taken to the emergency vet or need extra care from your regular vet. Trying saving $10 to $20 a month in an account for them so you will be prepared for any such emergencies.

Unless you plan to breed the Norwegian Forest cat that you adopt, you should spay or neuter your cat to help keep it in good health. For males, neutering can help prevent later behavioral problems, such as spraying urine, aggression, running away and it can help prevent testicular and mammary cancer.

Spaying females will prevent unwanted pregnancy, as well as spraying urine and it helps prevent uterine, ovarian and mammary cancers. It will also prevent pyometritis, which is a potentially fatal uterine infection that can happen about a week after a female has gone into heat.

In addition, a neutered or spayed cat will be less likely to want to go outside. If they do wish to go outdoors, try to create a fenced in area to keep them safe when they are outside. Screening in your patio with plastic chicken wire is a good option because it allows you cat to get some fresh air and sunshine, but they are in a safe environment.

Since Norwegian Forest cats love to climb and are skillful hunters, letting them roam free, even in a fenced in yard, could be dangerous. They will probably climb the fence or a tree and get out of the yard where they would be in danger from other stray cats, dog attacks, if they wander into the street they could be hit by vehicles or your cat could be bitten by an insect, which can transfer diseases to them.

Chapter 11 - Are You Ready to Adopt a Cat?

Adopting and properly caring for a cat is a big responsibility, which shouldn't be taken lightly. Cats cannot care for themselves and a people oriented breed like the Wegie will require you to spend some time with them.

However, if you have the time and are financially able to properly care for a Norwegian Forest cat, you will be rewarded many times over with their affection and love. The bond between a cat and its human is special and well worth the effort you put into your cat.

Chapter 12 - Clicker Training for Your Cat

Many people assume that cats want nothing to do with being trained or taught tricks and think they would be too stubborn to learn. However, most cats are very willing to learn and, with patience, you can correct their behaviors and teach them tricks.

Whether you are trying to correct your cat's behavior or teach it a trick, a Norwegian Forest cat loves spending time with their human and can be easily trained. They are a very intelligent breed and will easily learn what you are trying to teach them.

One of the best training methods to use for cats is clicker training. This type of training, more formerly called operant conditioning, uses a reward system to train cats, rather than punishment.

When you indicate a behavior that you want your cat to learn with a click, it should be given a treat when it repeats the preferred behavior.

The clicker used for training is a small plastic device that creates a clicking sound when the metal strip on the bottom of the device is pressed. The clicker is used because it is a distinctive sound that will generate curiosity the first time you use it. Voice commands can be added later, but in general, voice commands don't work well for training because they hear your voice everyday and it usually doesn't generate curiosity in your cat.

When you start training your cat using the clicker, he or she will quickly associate a click with the behavior you want them to repeat. Once it has made that association, they will repeat the behavior when they hear the click. It takes patience to train a cat, so don't get too anxious if they don't respond to the first, or even the second, time you show it the behavior you wish for it to repeat.

This process is often referred to as "charging the clicker." Giving your cat a treat after they have repeated the behavior will reinforce a positive consequence for their obedience, helping to make it easier to train.

Before you begin training, do some research online or buy a book that can help you get started with clicker training. Setting goals for your training is important as well. Decide which behaviors need to be replaced, which to encourage and decide if you wish to use the training to teach your cat tricks. Be reasonable when you set the goals and, above all, be patient as you begin the training.

The first step to clicker training is getting your cat used to the sound of the clicker. Since they need to associate the sound with a behavior, don't randomly use the clicker, use it only for training purposes.

Begin training by clicking it and immediately give your cat a treat. Be sure to use something they love to eat as this will help inspire them to participate in the training. Commercial cat treats work well for clicker training, but make sure they like the treats. When you give your cat a treat, you can either toss it to them or hand feed it to him or her.

Although it can take time for some cats to make the connection between the click and a treat, your Norwegian Forest cat is very smart and they should make the association quickly.

Once your cat understands that if they respond to the clicker, they will be rewarded with a treat, you can begin them on more advanced training. However, don't start it unless they have clearly made the association between the click and receiving the treat.

One of the easiest commands to teach a cat using clicker training is to come to you when they are called. Just as they would respond to the sound of a can opener, when you use the clicker, they will learn to come out of hiding in order to get their treat. The clicker can be useful when you cannot find them in the house and you need your cat to come to you.

Since the Wegie is such a smart breed, you may also be able to teach your cat how to respond to visual and vocal cues. Use the clicker to teach them the behavior, then associate the visual or vocal cue with the clicker and treat. Repeat the process until you can replace the clicker with the visual or vocal cue, but remember to reward their repetition of the behavior with a treat just as you did with the clicker.

Timing is important when you use clicker training and you want to try to time the clicking with the preferred behavior and not click after it.

If you click after you cat has started doing the behavior, they may abruptly stop and expect to be rewarded with a treat. As you continue working with your cat, he or she should repeat the preferred behavior before they get a treat.

Don't use more than one click while you are training your cat or you could confuse it. In addition, do not play with the clicker between training sessions because not only do you risk confusing them, but also they will be disappointed when they don't receive a treat after you use the clicker. The treat is to keep them interested in training, so don't click if you don't intend to reward your cat.

Start your cat's training with something easy that your cat is likely to do on its own. If they nuzzle your hand, use their scratching post or sit down, click during the act and then give him or her a treat. Your Wegie will quickly associate the behavior with the click and treat, then before you know it, he or she will repeat the behavior on command when they hear the click.

Keep each training session short so you don't get frustrated and your cat doesn't get bored. As they make progress toward the goals you've set for their training, be sure to reward them. Rewarding your cat as they make progress will let him or her know that it is doing the right thing and he or she will repeat the behavior in order to receive their tasty treat.

The key to training your Norwegian Forest cat is patience and rewarding them. Wegies love food and they are intelligent, which makes them easier to train than most other cat breeds. Once they have been taught two or three tricks, you can impress your family and friends with your well-behaved cat.

Chapter 13 - Showing Off Your Norwegian Forest Cat

Some breeders of purebred cats strive to produce the best cat breed they can and show them at cat shows all across the country and, sometimes, around the world. It isn't only breeders that show their cats, but owners do as well.

If you wish to put your Norwegian Forest cat in a show, you will need to become acquainted with the rules for cat shows and learn how the cats at the shows are judged.

In the United States, there are several organizations that sponsor cat shows. The American Association of Cat Enthusiasts (AACE), the Cat Fanciers' Association, (CFA), the American Cat Fanciers' Association (ACFA) and The International Cat Association (TICA) are the major organizations that regularly host cat shows in the U.S. and TICA also sponsors them around the world.

To help you learn about cat shows, you should attend a few in your area in order to help you determine if you want to put your cat, not to mention yourself, through all of the necessary training.

It can take several weeks, sometimes months, to properly prepare a cat for a show. If you are new to the cat show scene, attending cat shows and talking to some of the breeders, will help you understand what sort of preparations you will need to make and you may even make some connections.

A show cat will need to get used to being handled by judges and spending extended amounts of time in pens while waiting to be evaluated. Appearances are very important at shows and grooming needs to be done regularly.

Show cats need to be groomed daily and their claws should be clipped the day before a show. Your cat should be fed a healthy diet in order to be in good health and help them maintain the perfect weight for their body structure.

Your cat's vaccinations must be up-to-date or you will not be able to put them in a show. If your cat's shots are due near the date of a show, it is recommended that you have them vaccinated about 14 days prior to the show in case they have any reactions to the vaccines. Vaccinations are important since they will be exposed to other cats and it will help keep them from contracting an airborne illness.

To find show schedules, go online to each of the organizations' websites to view the schedules or you can request a schedule from them. Fill out the entry forms for the shows where you want to show your cat and mail them in, allowing plenty of time to process the forms so nothing goes wrong on the day of the show. The entry forms should have the closing date for entries listed on it or you can check with the shows' managers for the information.

Placing your Wegie in a cat show means that you need to teach your cat to travel well, whether you are driving or flying. As they will be required to stay in a pen for long periods of time at the show, you should be able to easily train them to travel in a cat carrier.

The cats in a show are separated into four classes:

The Kitten Class - Kittens must be at least 14 weeks old to be shown, but less than 10 months.

The Neuter Class - This class is for altered cats and they are judged by the same breed standards as unaltered cats.

The Open Class - This class is open to all cat breeds.

The Household Pet Class - This class is for cats that are altered and of unknown breed origin or who are unregistered. There are no breed standards used in this class and the cats are judged by their unique qualities.

Your Norwegian Forest cat, if not neutered or spayed, would be shown in the Open Class.

When it is time for your cat to be judged, one of the judges will physically and visually examine your cat. It will award points based on the breed standard for the Norwegian Forest cat.

The maximum number of points they can be awarded is 100 and the points are based on an examination of the symmetry of their head, the shape and structure of their body and tail, its coat, the color and/or markings, and the cat's balance.

For the Wegie, all colors and markings are allowable with or without white, unless it is a hybridization that results in the colors chocolate, lavender/lilac, a pointed pattern or a combination of those mixed with white.

(*Source:* "For more information on the breed standard for a
Norwegian Forest cat, the information is found on the TICA
website and reproduced below
http://www.tica.org/members/publications/standards/nf.pdf

NORWEGIAN FOREST (NF)

HEAD . . . . 40 points

Shape 8
Ears 8
Eyes 8
Chin 4
Muzzle 4
Profile 8

BODY . . . . 35 points

Torso 7
Legs 7
Tail 7
Boning 7
Musculature 7

COAT AND COLOR . . . . 25 points

Length 5
Texture 20

CATEGORY: Traditional.

DIVISION: All Divisions.

COLORS: All Colors.

PERMISSIBLE OUTCROSSES:

None.

HEAD:

Shape: Triangular, where all sides are equally long when measured from the outer base of the ears to the chin and between the outer base of the ears; good height when seen in profile; forehead is sloped back.

Eyes: Large, almond shaped, set obliquely. Alert expression. All eye colors except odd-eyes or blue permitted regardless of coat color.

Odd-eyes and blue eyes permitted in white and with white only.

Ears: Large, wide at the base, arched forward as if listening, slightly rounded tips that appear pointed when lynx tips are present. Lynx tips and furnishings that extend beyond the outer edge of each ear are desirable. The outer edge of the ear should follow the line of the head down to the chin.

Muzzle: Following the line of the triangular head, with no evidence of pinch or snippiness.

Profile: Long, straight profile from tip of nose to brow without break in line, i.e., no stop.

Neck: Muscular; medium in length.

BODY:

Torso: Medium long and substantial.

Legs: In proportion to the body length, with hind legs higher than fore legs.

Feet: Large, round, well-tufted. Tail: Long and bushy. Should be

at least as long as the body. Boning: Substantial.

Musculature: Strongly built and sturdy.

COAT/COLOR:

Length: Semi-long.

Texture: The dense, woolly undercoat is covered by a smooth, water repellant upper coat which consists of long, coarse and glossy hair covering the back and the sides. A fully coated cat has a full ruff and britches.

Colors: All colors of all divisions of the traditional category are recognized including all colors with white. Any amount of white is allowed anywhere on the cat.

OTHER:

Balance: Muscular and well- proportioned.

Condition: Not applicable/ assumed.

Temperament: Intelligent and independent.

ALLOWANCES:

Buttons, spots and lockets allowed in all colors. Length of coat and density of undercoat vary with the seasons. Under no circumstances should a cat be penalized for having a semi-long coat. Coat is evaluated primarily on texture and quality. Allow for size difference between males and females. Very slow maturing of this breed should be taken into account.

Mature males may have broader heads than females.

PENALIZE:

Too small and finely built cats. Round or square head; profile with a break (stop). Round eyes. Ears too small or narrow at the base. Legs that are short, thin - not in proportion to the body, or cowhocked. Short tail. Cobby or extremely long body. Dry or silky texture on coat.

Temperament must be unchallenging; any sign of definite challenge shall disqualify. The cat may exhibit fear, seek to flee, or generally complain aloud but may not threaten to harm.

In accordance with Show Rules, ARTICLE SIXTEEN, the following shall be considered mandatory disqualifications: a cat that bites (216.9), a cat showing evidence of intent to deceive (216.10), adult whole male cats not having two descended testicles (216.11), cats with all or part of the tail missing , except as authorized by a board approved standard (216.12.1), cats with more than five toes on each front foot and four toes on each back foot, unless proved the result of an injury or as authorized by a Board approved standard (216.12.2), visible or invisible tail faults if

Board approved standard requires disqualification (216.12.4), crossed eyes if

Board approved standard requires disqualification (216.12.5), total blindness (216.12.6), markedly smaller size, not in keeping with the breed (216.12.9), and depression of the sternum or unusually small diameter of the rib cage itself (216.12.11.1). See Show Rules, ARTICLE SIXTEEN for more comprehensive rules governing penalties and disqualifications.

After your cat has been judged, they will write up a report that is forwarded to the show secretary. The results are recorded and the paperwork for the "Best in Show" nomination is prepared.

A cat can win its breed division and it can be nominated for "Best in Show" as well. The cats that have been nominated for "Best in Show" will be taken before a panel of judges, who will examine them once again. Afterwards, they will vote on "Best in Show."

Even if your cat doesn't do well in a show, you will have several opportunities to show them again. If you plan to show your cat, you must be prepared to spend weeks or months working with them in order to make sure they are prepared for the process.

Chapter 13 - Showing Off Your Norwegian Forest Cat

Many people who show cats raise them specifically for that reason and they may breed them as well. It can be a lot of work for both you and your Wegie, but showing him or her can be a rewarding experience.

Chapter 14 - Traveling with Your Cat

Chapter 14 - Traveling with Your Cat

Traveling with a cat can be challenging, especially if you are driving in a vehicle. Most cats are not fond of being in a moving vehicle, unless they have been taught to get used to it from a young age or they are an extraordinary cat.

Even though you may try to acclimate your cat to riding in a car when they are young, some cats never get used to it and do not enjoy the experience.

Unless your Norwegian Forest cat has been trained to ride in a car, and likes the experience, you should always put your cat in a sturdy cat carrier when you go to the vet or on a trip. While you can use a soft-sided carrier, they are really made for airplane travel and it is better to use a hard-sided carrier when you're in a car.

The sturdier carrier gives them a bit more room to move around, especially as they are a bigger breed of cat, but it can also help protect your cat in case of an accident.

If you are traveling a short distance, such as to the vet, you may not need to make any extra preparations for your cat. However, if you are taking them on a longer trip, you will need to take some cat essentials along.

Traveling with a pet is much like traveling with a child, you need to take some supplies in order to make the trip more comfortable for them by keeping them calm.

Line their carrier with a blanket or a towel to give them something soft to cuddle up in, especially if you are traveling during the cooler months. A Norwegian Forest cat can easily withstand cold weather, but they would still like to have something soft on which to lie.

Take water, food, bowls, a litter pan and litter on the trip to accommodate their needs. Place their favorite small toys in the carrier with them for both comfort and to give them something to pass the time.

The best place to put the carrier is in the middle of the back seat. This placement will prevent the sun from shining directly onto the carrier, which can make the trip uncomfortably warm for your Wegie.

Secure the carrier with a seatbelt to keep it from sliding around on the seat in case you have to make a sudden stop or swerve the car. If the carrier isn't secure, your cat can be injured if the carrier overturns.

Some cats have motion sickness and it can be worsened if they can see outside during the trip. To help prevent their motion sickness, place their carrier on the floorboard behind one of the front seats. Try to prevent the floor air blower from directly blowing onto the carrier, especially if you have the heater on because it can get too hot for a thick furred Wegie.

On a longer trip, you should set up a litter box inside of your vehicle. A covered litter pan works best because it will prevent the litter from spilling onto the floor of your vehicle.

Unlike dogs, your cat doesn't need to stretch its legs on a trip until you stop for the night. It is important that you keep your cat in its carrier while traveling, especially when you stop so that it doesn't bolt out of the car and get lost in unfamiliar territory.

Traveling on an airplane has its own unique issues for you and your pet. Before you take them with you on a plane, you need to contact the airline to find out their pet policy before purchasing a ticket. Although it is faster to look for their policy on their website, policies are subject to change and you may wish to contact them directly to confirm the information on their site. Most airlines allow pets to be carried on the plane, which is what you should do with your cat.

A soft-sided pet carrier will fit under the seat in front of you, but you can also buy the seat beside you and place a hard-sided carrier on it. As you would when traveling by car, take some things with you to help comfort them. Place a blanket and their favorite toy in the carrier with them so they can snuggle while traveling.

You will need to get a health certificate from your cat's vet before traveling by plane. The airline will want to see that your cat has been vaccinated before you can take it on the plane. Keep the health certificate with you at all times so it is easily accessible. Put a collar on your cat with an identification tag with his or her name, your telephone number and address in case your cat manages to escape the carrier.

If you are traveling internationally on vacation, it would be better to have a trusted friend or family member look after your cat while you're away than it would be to try to take your cat with you.

Unless you are moving to another country, making arrangements for a pet can be a hassle on short international trips. Some countries will not allow foreign animals into their country, while other countries require them to be quarantined on arrival. It can take weeks, if not months, to get approval to take your pet into another country.

Some cats may require a visit to their vet before you take your trip. Some of them need to be sedated because they do not travel well due to car or air-sickness. Always check with your veterinarian before giving your cat anything to keep it calm.

Some sedatives or tranquilizers will affect cat's body temperature or they may have other adverse reactions to them, even if they are made from natural herbs. It is better to let your vet sedate them or advise you on which sedative is best for your cat.

By being properly prepared and by taking the supplies your cat needs along on the trip, you can enjoy traveling with your cat. Work with your Wegie to train them to lie calmly in a carrier so they will be used to it when it is time to take them on a trip. Start with small car rides across town and gradually make them longer so your cat will get used to car travel. They may never like it, but with patience and preparation, the travel experience will be better for you and your cat.

Chapter 15 - Breeding Your Norwegian Forest Cat

Even though you may love your Norwegian Forest cat and wish to breed him or her to produce a litter of kittens, cat breeding isn't something that should be considered lightly. If you get your cat intending to breed it, you should do so responsibly and with a full understanding of the cat breeding process. Breeding your cat for the fun of having kittens in the house or to make money from the kittens are poor reasons for getting into the business It's also the reason why there are so many disreputable breeders.

Since the Norwegian Forest cat was on the brink of extinction at one point, many breeders are devoted to keeping the breed alive and making sure they remain a healthy, hardy breed of cat. They want them to be around for future generations to enjoy, but they want future cat generations to remain healthy and strong as well. These breeders run reputable catteries and many of them show their cats in order to promote the breed.

Breeding and caring for cats is a time consuming and expensive undertaking. Before you decide to get into the business, you should talk with other breeders and read everything you can on breeding before you consider producing a litter of kittens. You will need to learn how to properly care for a pregnant queen, which is the term used for the female that is bred, and properly care for the kittens, which includes finding them good homes.

To produce the best possible offspring for the breed, your cat should display excellent breed standards and be in excellent health. It is important to be committed and involved with the kittens that are produced, preferably throughout their lives. It is the breeder's responsibility to see that the kittens are prepared for adoption and that they are placed in good homes. There are already too many unwanted kittens in the world and you don't want to add to the population.

Both the male and female cat should be allowed to reach maturity before they are bred. Females can be bred starting at 18 to 24 months old, but if they are bred before 18 months of age, they will not have the opportunity to finish growing because they will put all of their energy into taking care of and nourishing the kittens.

Male cats should also be at least 18 months old before they are used for breeding. They need to reach maturity to make sure their temperament makes them suitable for breeding and that they are healthy. The male's temperament can be passed on to its offspring, just as genetic diseases can, and you don't want to produce kittens that are aggressive or shy if you can prevent that possibility.

If you intend to breed Norwegian Forest cats, you should get kittens from unrelated litters to use as the tom and the queen. This will keep your line of Wegies from being inner-bred and help ensure a healthy line. Owning both the tom and the queen will be more convenient for you and ensure that both cats are healthy and well cared for before any kittens are produced.

Before the breeding begins, your vet should give your cats a thorough examination, check the stools for parasites and make sure their vaccinations are up-to-date. The cats should be as healthy as possible before being bred to keep any illnesses or diseases from being passed on to their offspring. The tom and queen should also be free of ear mites, ringworm and fleas.

Both parents need to be tested and certified that they are free from the feline leukemia virus (FeLV) and the feline immunodeficiency virus (FIV). Have the cats tested for the genetic diseases that the Norwegian Forest cat can have, such as hypertrophic cardiomyopathy, glycogen storage disease type IV, hip or retinal dysplasia. A responsible breeder will not breed their cats if they test positive for any of these conditions, but will spay or neuter them instead.

It is important for the queen to be at her ideal weight before she conceives. If she is too thin or too heavy, she can have problems getting pregnant, carrying a litter or queening, which means giving birth. By feeding her a proper diet, you can keep both the queen and the tom in good health and at their ideal weight throughout their lives.

If you adopt Wegies with the intention of breeding them, select your tom and queen very carefully. Make sure they are healthy and have been well cared for, which will help ensure that they produce healthy kittens. Check their medical certifications, get to know their personalities and adopt cats with the best breed standards that you can. If you are careful in selecting your cats, they are more likely to produce healthy, friendly Norwegian Forest kittens.

Chapter 16 - Caring for the Queen During Pregnancy

Once your male and female Norwegian Forest cats are at least 18 months old, they are ready to be bred. The queen will go into heat during certain seasons of the year, which is called being seasonally polyestrous. If females are not bred, they will cycle many times. Cats also need to breed before ovulation as they are reflex ovulators. Indoor cats, which are exposed to artificial light, can cycle year-round, while outdoor cats usually cycle in the spring and summer months.

There are five stages to a cat's heat, or estrous, cycle:

Anestrus

Proestrous

Estrus

Interfollicular

Metestrous

Anestrus

This stage usually occurs during the winter months. The tom will not be interested in the queen during this stage nor will the queen be attracted to the tom.

Proestrous

This stage occurs before the queen goes into heat. During this stage, she may "call" to the tom, roll around and/or rub on the ground. However, she usually will not let the tom approach her yet. Female cats do not bleed during this time like other animals. The proestrous stage can progress into the estrous stage in just a few hours.

Estrus

The estrus stage will last for about a week and the queen should be mated during this time, which is when she will allow the tom approach her.

Mating lasts from one to 20 seconds and the tom should have an escape route to get away from the queen as she may respond aggressively after mating. Use a box or make sure there is a shelf nearby that the tom can jump to immediately after he has mated with the queen.

You can tell the queen has mated because she will thoroughly groom herself and not be approachable for about an hour. Afterwards, the tom can approach again and they will resume mating. To help ensure that the queen gets pregnant, allow her to mate three times a day for the first three days of estrus. Studies show that it helps produce ovulation in 90% of queens.

If she mated successfully, gestation will last for 63 days. You can determine her due day by adding 63 days to each she was bred. However, if for some reason she aborts or loses her nursing kittens, the queen will return to the estrus stage within two to three weeks. She will be ready to be bred again, if you desire.

The first sign of pregnancy is the lack of heat cycles. It can be difficult to tell if a queen is pregnant during the first two to three weeks of her pregnancy. Several methods can be used to determine if the queen is pregnant.

An ultrasound can be done to check for fetuses at days 14 or 15, your veterinarian will be able to feel the fetuses with abdominal palpations around days 17 or 18 and heartbeats using an ultrasound are detectable starting at day 24.

The most accurate way to determine a pregnancy is to have the queen x-rayed around days 43 to 45. The fetal skeletons can be seen at that time, but the later the x-rays are taken, the more accurate they will be. Nothing physical is discernable until around the 5th week of pregnancy, which is when the queen's abdomen will start to enlarge, but if her litter is small, it will take longer for her to show.

Once a pregnancy is confirmed, the queen should be started on a vitamin and mineral supplement by your vet. Your vet can make sure you are adequately feeding the queen and the supplement will help ensure she is getting a well balanced diet.

Be careful not to over-supplement the queen as it can adversely affect the developing kittens. The queen should exercise as she normally would to keep her from gaining too much weight and to maintain her muscle tone.

If she was on a premium cat food before her pregnancy, it should be maintained for the first few weeks of her pregnancy. At about the fourth week of her pregnancy, you should add a high-quality kitten food to her diet.

Each week you will increase the amount of kitten food in her diet until the final week, when she should be eating nothing but kitten food. This helps to provide all of the vitamins and minerals the kittens will need to be at their healthiest when they are born.

The queen's meal frequency should be increased to three times a day by the middle of her pregnancy, around day 30, and you can allow her to free feed during this time. During the last week of pregnancy, she may need to eat small meals every three to four hours as the kittens continue to grow. Kittens grow the most during their last two weeks of gestation.

During the last week of her pregnancy, as well as the first three to four weeks of lactating, you can increase the amount of food she eats. It can be increased to one and a half to twice the amount of food she ate before the pregnancy. As long as she maintains a healthy weight during lactation, the queen should be able to have the extra food, which she will need to keep up her energy levels and properly nourish her kittens.

If possible, all medications should be avoided during pregnancy and lactation. The only time medications that are harmful to developing fetuses should be administered is to save the queen's life. For any medications or supplements, consult with your vet before you give them to the queen to check if they are harmful to her kittens.

About two weeks before her due date, you should set-up a nesting box for the queen. Something as simple as a cardboard box or a laundry basket works well for a nesting box. Line it with a blanket or towels to create a soft area for the queen and her kittens. Setting it up in advance will allow the queen to become accustomed to the nesting area before she goes into labor.

If you want to be present during labor, start taking the queen's temperature about two weeks before her due date. Lubricate the thermometer with KY jelly or margarine so it is easy to insert into her rectum. Insert it about a half inch and let it remain there for three minutes. You will probably have to hold the thermometer in place because the queen isn't going to be too pleased with this treatment.

The temperature should read between 101 and 102 degrees Fahrenheit, but it will drop to 100 degrees just before she goes into labor. When her temperature drops, the queen should start to deliver her litter about 24 hours later. There are other signs of impending labor that will begin within 24 to 48 hours before she goes into labor.

The queen may seem anxious and start looking for a place to have her litter. When she begins this behavior, confine her to the room where you want her to have the kittens. The room should be darkened and in a quiet area in order to make her feel that it is safe for her kittens. Be sure to keep fresh water, food and a clean litter box in the room at all times.

Just before she begins labor, the queen may also start to repeatedly lick her abdomen and vagina. She may have a discharge prior to birth, but you may not see it as she will lick it away. She will be dilating at this time, but you won't see any outward signs of it. Don't check her vagina, just leave her alone during this time.

Her breath rate may increase and she may cry out or pace while she is in labor. As her contractions begin, the queen will lie on her side, then get up and squat while pressing down to drop her kittens. You can watch from a distance, but do not interrupt or disturb her while she is in the process of having her kittens. The first kitten should emerge about an hour after she begins laboring.

Labor may only take a few minutes before the first kitten arrives and the next one will arrive within 10 minutes to an hour later. The remaining kittens in the litter will arrive within the same time intervals. They come out wrapped in a membrane, so the queen will immediately start licking her kitten to open the sac and allow the kitten to breathe. The licking also helps to stimulate the kitten's circulation and respiration.

If she cannot break through the sac or doesn't do so, you will need to gently, but vigorously rub the kitten using a soft cloth to get the membrane off it and allow them to breathe. Place the kitten at a nipple because the queen will immediately start nursing her kittens after she chews away the umbilical cord and before the rest of the litter arrives. Nursing helps to stimulate further contractions.

If you need to help cut any umbilical cords the queen has forgotten to take care of, gently tie a piece of string or dental flows around the kitten's umbilical cord and snip it about an inch long. It usually takes two to six hours for her entire litter to be delivered. If it takes longer than seven hours, gather her and the kittens and take them to the vet.

After she is finished having her litter, you can quietly clean up after her. Place her food and water nearby because she will not want to leave her kittens unattended for too long for the first couple of days. Leave her in the birthing room, keeping it dark and as quiet as possible so as not to disturb the new family. If you take good care of the queen before and during her pregnancy, as well as labor, she will be more likely to have a healthy litter of kittens.

Chapter 17 - Raising Healthy, Happy Kittens

You have a lot of work ahead of you once the kittens have arrived. Though there isn't much you can do for the kittens during their first few days, as the queen will see to their care, you can ensure that the room they are in stays warm enough for them.

Kittens cannot regulate their body temperatures for their first few weeks, so the room needs to stay between 75 and 80 degrees Fahrenheit for the first week. Then the temperature can gradually be reduced to 70 degrees.

If you need to have a heat source in the room, do not let it be any warmer than the queen, as the kittens will gravitate toward it to nurse. Kittens usually lay on their sides or atop their littermates to stay warm and to keep in contact with them. If the kittens are spread out, they are probably too warm. A kitten's normal temperature is around 97 degrees Fahrenheit and it will gradually climb each week until it reaches 100.5 to 102.5, which is the same as an adult cat, at around four weeks old.

A healthy kitten is plump, they have a firm body and they are lively. They usually nurse about every one to two hours and their tiny stomachs appear rounded, then they will sleep quietly. If you see them moving around more than usual or crying, they may not be getting enough to eat. Swallowing air will make their stomachs appear as they would if they were nursing normally. As they weaken, they will stop moving and crying.

If they don't appear to be feeding well or getting enough to eat, take the queen and the kittens to the veterinarian. You may need to intercede and hand feed a kitten that is having problems nursing or isn't getting enough to eat.

Kittens that are not thriving should be taken to the vet in order to diagnose any possible genetic diseases or birth defects. Some defects, such as a cleft palate, are not compatible with life and they will be humanely euthanized.

Kittens normally weigh between 90 and 100 grams at birth. Those weighing less than 90 grams may expire within a few days after their birth. Although kittens may lose a small amount of weight about 24 hours after their birth, they normally gain 7 to 10 grams per day. Their weight should double within the first 14 days of their life. It is important to track the kittens' weight every day for the first two weeks and then two to three times a week until they are weaned. Failure to gain weight is a sign of illness in kittens.

As they nurse, you may notice that the kittens are at the same teat each time they feed. Kittens prefer to use the same teat when they nurse, which they will pick out during the first few days of life.

They use their sense of smell to find their preferred teat when it is time to nurse. While they are nursing, the queen will lick their stomachs and perineal area to stimulate their ability to urinate and defecate. She will continue to do so for the first two to three weeks of their life.

Check the queen's mammary glands and nipples once a day to look for redness, hardness, streaking color or discharge. An infection of a mammary gland, called mastitis, needs to be immediately treated.

Sometimes the infection can be milked out and using hot compresses on the infected area may help to keep the infection from spreading. Antibiotics may be necessary as well. If there is mastitis in several glands, the kittens may need to be hand fed.

Grooming the kittens starts at an early age because their tiny claws will need to be kept trim so they don't scratch the queen's mammary glands. Their nails should be trimmed starting within a few days of their birth and maintained weekly. This will also help them get used to having their nails trimmed and make it easier to do as they get older.

Kittens are born without teeth and their deciduous, or baby, teeth will start coming in at about two to four weeks of age. Around the second week of life, start checking the queen's mammary glands for bite marks as well as scratches. By the time kittens are eight weeks old, all of their baby teeth should be present. They will eventually lose these teeth, which will be replaced with their adult teeth.

Around three to four weeks of age, the kittens will start imitating the queen when she eats and drinks. You will need to keep a shallow bowl of water out for them, at least for part of the day.

At this time, you can start making kitten mush for them to eat. Kitten mush is a blend of high quality kitten food, replacement kitten milk and hot water. Blend it until it has the same consistency as human baby cereal so they can easily eat it.

At first, the kittens should be fed kitten mush three to four times a day. Once they have checked it out and eaten some of it, allow the queen to finish it and clean up her kittens. Each week decrease the amount of replacement milk and water in the mush and blend it less. By the time they are seven to 8 weeks old, they should be eating dry kitten food and be fully weaned from the teat.

Clean and change out the nesting box at least once a day as the kittens will be urinating and defecating in it for the first few weeks of their lives. At around four weeks old, they will start behavior that looks as if they are scratching at sand.

They will start following the queen to the litter box and, although they may just play in it at first, around six weeks of age, they will learn how to potty in it. They will learn to bury their feces by watching the queen and they then will need access to a litter pan with shorter sides so they can easily climb in and out of it.

As the queen starts to spend more time away from the kittens, they will start to follow her and explore their world. It is important to supervise them as they explore so they aren't lost or injured. Give them soft toys to play with and, if they fall asleep in odd places, return them to their box to rest. The queen will probably take them herself, but you can occasionally lend her a helping hand.

For the most part, kittens learn from the queen by imitating her actions. They will learn how to eat, how to use the litter box, hunt and they will learn to fear what she fears. Since the Norwegian Forest cat is a mild-mannered, fearless and fun loving breed, you can expect the kittens to turn out the same way.

Conclusion

Thank you again for buying this book! I spent months writing it. As someone who has loved these cats for years, friends told me to share my knowledge!

I hope this book helped you decide if the Norwegian Forest breed is right for your home and to learn how to raise it properly.

Please Help....

Finally, if you enjoyed this book, please, please, please take the time to share your thoughts and post a review on whatever site you purchased it from. It will be greatly appreciated!

The biggest criticism is always going to be making a book specific to the 'Norwegian Forest' I have tried where possible to show you how this breed is unique and why it is different. But equally it does share similarities with other breeds.

Index

Index

Index

Index